Software Distribution Using the ESP Package Manager

MICHAEL R. SWEET

ESP Press

Easy Software Products, 516 Rio Grand Ct, Morgan Hill, CA 95037 USA

Software Distribution Using the ESP Package Manager

Copyright © 2006-2010 by Easy Software Products

This book was created solely using free software tools.

International Standard Book Number: 978-1-4116-8913-8

First Printing: April 2006
Second Printing: December 2010

Table of Contents

Table of Contents

Preface

This book provides a tutorial and reference for the ESP Package Manager ("EPM") software, version 4.2, and is organized into the following chapters and appendices:

- 1 - Introduction to EPM
- 2 - Building EPM
- 3 - Packaging Your Software with EPM
- 4 - Advanced Packaging with EPM
- 5 - EPM Packaging Examples
- A - Software License Agreement
- B - Command Reference
- C - List File Reference
- D - Release Notes

Notation Conventions

The names of commands; the first mention of a command or
function in a chapter is followed by a manual page section
number:

```
epm
epm(1)
```

File and directory names:

/var
/usr/bin/epm

Screen output:

```
Request ID is Printer-123
```

Literal user input; special keys like ENTER are in ALL CAPS:

```
lp -d printer filename ENTER
```

Long commands are broken up on multiple lines using the
backslash (\) character; enter the commands without the
backslash:

```
foo start of long command \
    end of long command ENTER
```

Numbers in the text are written using the period (.) to
indicate the decimal point:

12.3

Abbreviations

The following abbreviations are used throughout this book:

kb
Kilobytes, or 1024 bytes

Mb
Megabytes, or 1048576 bytes

Gb
Gigabytes, or 1073741824 bytes

Other References

http://www.epmhome.org/
The official home page of the ESP Package Manager software.

http://www.debian.org/devel/
Debian Developers' Corner

http://techpubs.sgi.com/
IRIX Documentation On-Line

http://www.rpm.org/
The Red Hat Package Manager home page.

http://docs.sun.com/
Solaris Documentation On-Line

Help Us Improve This Book!

We've done our best to ensure that this book is both accurate and clear. If you find errors or have a suggestion for improving the book, please send us an email to "epm-book@easysw.com".

Acknowledgments

We'd like to thank the following people for their contributions to EPM:

- Gareth Armstrong: HP-UX and %release enhancements
- Nicolas Bazin: Openserver and Unixware support
- Richard Begg: HP-UX fixes
- Dirk Datzert: Bug fixes
- Alan Eldridge: Makefile and RPM fixes
- Vicentini Emanuele: IRIX enhancements
- Jeff Harrell: IRIX enhancements
- Lars Kellogg-Stedman: Debian fixes
- Jochen Kmietsch: mkepmlist fixes
- Aneesh Kumar K.V.: Tru64 setld package support
- David Lee: Build system improvements
- Scott Leerssen: mkepmlist fixes, BSD package support
- Jeff Licquia: Debian support/enhancements
- David Maltz: AIX fixes
- Joel Nordell: SCO fixes
- Rok Papez: Bug fixes and absolute output directory support
- Holger Paschke: Documentation fixes
- Phil Reynolds: OpenBSD fixes
- Ganesan Rajagopal: Solaris fixes
- Uwe Räsche: AIX support
- Ralf Rohm: Solaris fixes
- Jochen Schaeuble: epminstall fixes
- Jason Shiffer: HP-UX fixes
- Andrea Suatoni: IRIX fixes
- Andy Walter: QNX support
- Geoffrey Wossum: --output-directory option
- Jean Yves: BSD package and mkepmlist fixes

1 - Introduction to EPM

This chapter provides an introduction to the ESP Package Manager ("EPM").

What is EPM?

Software distribution under UNIX/Linux can be a challenge, especially if you ship software for more than one operating system. Every operating system provides its own software packaging tools and each has unique requirements or implications for the software development environment.

The ESP Package Manager ("EPM") is one solution to this problem. Besides its own "portable" distribution format, EPM also supports the generation of several vendor-specific formats. This allows you to build software distribution files for almost any operating system from the same sources.

History and Evolution

When Easy Software Products was founded in 1993, we originally shipped software only for the SGI IRIX operating system. In 1997 we added support for Solaris, which was quickly followed by HP-UX support in 1998.

Each new operating system and supported processor required a new set of packaging files. While this worked, it also meant that we had to keep all of the packaging files synchronized manually. Needless to say, this process was far from perfect and we had more than one distribution that was not identical on all operating systems.

As we began developing CUPS (http://www.cups.org/) in 1997, our initial goal was to add support for two additional operating systems: Linux and Compaq Tru64 UNIX. If we wanted to avoid the mistakes of the past, we clearly had to change how we produced software distributions.

The first version of EPM was released in 1999 and supported so-called "portable" software distributions that were not tied to any particular operating system or packaging software. Due to popular demand, we added support for vendor-specific packaging formats in the second major release of EPM, allowing the generation of portable or "native" distributions from one program and one set of software distribution files.

Existing Software Packaging Systems

As we looked for a solution to our problem, we naturally investigated the existing open-source packaging systems. Under Linux, we looked at the Red Hat Package Manager ("RPM") and Debian packaging software ("dpkg" and "dselect"). For the commercial UNIX's we looked at the vendor-supplied packaging systems. Table 1.1 shows the results of our investigation.

Table 1.1: Software Packaging Formats

Format	Operating Systems1	Binaries	Cross-Platform	Patches	Up-grades	Con-flicts	Re-quires	Re-places	Config Files	Map Files	Un-install
installp	AIX	Yes	No	No	No	Yes	Yes	No	No	No	Yes
pkg_add	FreeBSD	Yes	Yes2	No	No	No	No	No	No	No	Yes
pkg_add	NetBSD OpenBSD	Yes	Yes2	No	No	Yes	Yes	No	No	No	Yes
dpkg	Corel Linux Debian GNU/Linux	Yes	Yes2	No	Yes	Yes	Yes	Yes	Yes	No	Yes
depot	HP-UX	Yes	No	Yes	Yes	Yes	Yes	No	Yes	Yes	Yes
inst	IRIX	Yes	No	Yes	Yes	Yes	Yes	Yes	Yes	Yes	Yes
Install.app	MacOS X	Yes	No	No	Yes	No	No	No	No	No	No
pkgadd	Solaris	Yes	No	Yes	No	Yes	Yes	No	Yes	Yes	Yes
rpm	Mandrake Red Hat SuSE TurboLinux	Yes	Yes2	No	Yes	Yes	Yes	No	Yes	No	Yes
setld	Tru64 UNIX	Yes	No	No	No	Yes	Yes	No	No	No	Yes
slackware	Slackware Linux	Yes	No	No	No	Yes	Yes	No	No	No	Yes

1. Standard packaging system for named operating systems.
2. These packaging systems are cross-platform but require the package management utilities to be installed on the platform before installing the package.

As you can see, none of the formats supported every feature we were looking for. One common fault of all these formats is that they do not support a common software specification file format. That is, making a Debian software distribution requires significantly different support files than required for a Solaris pkg distribution. This makes it extremely difficult to manage distributions for multiple operating systems.

All of the package formats support binary distributions. The RPM and Debian formats also support source distributions that specifically allow for recompilation and installation. Only the commercial UNIX formats support patch distributions - you have to completely upgrade a software package with RPM and Debian. All but the Solaris pkg format allow you to upgrade a package without removing the old version first.

When building the software packages, RPM and Debian force you to create the actual directories, copy the files to those directories, and set the ownerships and permissions. You essentially are creating a directory for your software that can be archived in the corresponding package format. To ensure that all file permissions and ownerships are correct, you must build the distribution as the root user or use the fakeroot software, introducing potential security risks and violating many corporate security policies. It can also make building distributions difficult when dynamic data such as changing data files or databases is involved.

The commercial UNIX formats use software list files that map source files to the correct directories and permissions. This allows for easier delivery of dynamic data, configuration management of what each distribution actually contains, and eliminates security issues with special permissions and building distributions as the root user. Using the proprietary format also has the added benefit of allowing for software patches and using the familiar software installation tools for that operating system. The primary disadvantage is that the same distributions and packaging software cannot be used on other operating systems.

Design Goals of EPM

EPM was designed from the beginning to build binary software distributions using a common software specification format. The same distribution files work for all operating systems and all distribution formats. Supporting source code distributions was not a goal since most RPM and Debian source distributions are little more than wrapping around a compressed tar file containing the source files and a configure script.

Over the years, additional features have made their way into EPM to support more advanced software packages. Whenever possible, EPM emulates a feature if the vendor package format does not support it natively.

Resources

The EPM web site provides access to the current software, documentation, and discussion forums for EPM:

```
http://www.epmhome.org/
```

The EPM source code can be downloaded in compressed tar files or via the popular Subversion software. Please see the EPM web site for complete instructions.

Send book feedback to "epm-book@easysw.com".

2 - Building EPM

This chapter shows how to configure, build, and install the ESP Package Manager.

Requirements

EPM requires very little pre-installed software to work. Most items will likely be provided as part of your OS. Your development system will need a C compiler, the make(1) program (GNU, BSD, and most vendor make programs should work), the Bourne (or Korn or Bash) shell (sh(1)), and gzip(1).

The optional graphical setup program requires a C++ compiler, the FLTK library, version 1.1.x, and (for UNIX/Linux) the X11 libraries. FLTK is available at the following URL:

```
http://www.fltk.org/
```

Your end-user systems will require the Bourne (or Korn or Bash) shell (sh), the df(1) program, the tar(1) program, and the gzip(1) program to install portable distributions. All but the last are standard items, and most vendors include gzip as well.

EPM can also generate vendor-specific distributions. These require the particular vendor tool, such as rpm(8) and dpkg(8), to generate the software distribution on the development system and load the software distribution on the end-user system.

Configuring the Software

EPM uses GNU autoconf(1) to configure itself for your system. The configure script is used to configure the EPM software, as follows:

```
./configure ENTER
```

Choosing Compilers

If the configure script is unable to determine the name of your C or C++ compiler, set the CC and CXX environment variables to point to the C and C++ compiler programs, respectively. You can set these variables using the following commands in the Bourne, Korn, or Bash shells:

```
export CC=/foo/bar/gcc ENTER
export CXX=/foo/bar/gcc ENTER
```

If you are using C shell or tcsh, use the following commands instead:

```
setenv CC /foo/bar/gcc ENTER
setenv CXX /foo/bar/gcc ENTER
```

Run the configure script again to use the new commands.

Choosing Installation Directories

The default installation prefix is */usr*, which will place the
EPM programs in */usr/bin*, the setup GUI in */usr/lib/epm*, and
the man pages in */usr/man*. Use the `--prefix` option to
relocate these files

to another directory:

```
./configure --prefix=/usr/local ENTER
```

The `configure` script also accepts the `--bindir`, `--libdir`, and
`--mandir` options to relocate each directory separately, as
follows:

```
./configure --bindir=/usr/local/bin --libdir=/usr/local/lib \
    --mandir=/usr/local/share/man ENTER
```

Options for the Setup GUI

The setup GUI requires the FLTK library. The configure script
will look for the `fltk-config` utility that comes with FLTK
1.1.x. Set the FLTKCONFIG environment variable to the full
path of this utility if it cannot be found in the current path:

```
setenv FLTKCONFIG /foo/bar/bin/fltk-config ENTER
```

or:

```
FLTKCONFIG=/foo/bar/bin/fltk-config ENTER
export FLTKCONFIG
```

Building the Software

Once you have configured the software, type the following
command to compile it:

```
make ENTER
```

Compilation should take a few minutes at most. Then type
the following command to determine if the software

compiled successfully:

```
make test ENTER
Portable distribution build test PASSED.
Native distribution build test PASSED.
```

The test target builds a portable and native distribution of EPM and reports if the two distributions were generated successfully.

Installing the Software

Now that you have compiled and tested the software, you can install it using the make command or one of the distributions that was created. You should be logged in as the super-user unless you specified installation directories for which you have write permission. The su(8) command is usually sufficient to install software:

```
su ENTER
```

Operating systems such as MacOS X do not enable the root account by default. The sudo(8) command is used instead:

```
sudo installation command ENTER
```

Installing Using the make Command

Type the following command to install the EPM software using the make command:

```
make install ENTER
Installing EPM setup in /usr/lib/epm
Installing EPM programs in /usr/bin
Installing EPM manpages in /usr/man/man1
Installing EPM documentation in /usr/share/doc/epm
```

Use the sudo command to install on MacOS X:

```
sudo make install ENTER
Installing EPM setup in /usr/lib/epm
Installing EPM programs in /usr/bin
Installing EPM manpages in /usr/man/man1
```

Installing Using the Portable Distribution

The portable distribution can be found in a subdirectory named using the operating system, version, and architecture. For example, the subdirectory for a Linux 2.4.x system on an Intel-based system would be *linux-2.4-intel*. The subdirectory name is built from the following template:

    os-major.minor-architecture

The os name is the common name for the operating system. Table 2.1 lists the abbreviations for most operating systems.

The major.minor string is the operating system version number. Any patch revision information is stripped from the version number, as are leading characters before the major version number. For example, HP-UX version B.11.11 will result in a version number string of 11.11.

Table 2.1: Operating System Name Abbreviations

Operating System	Name
AIX	aix
Compaq Tru64 UNIX Digital UNIX OSF/1	tru64
FreeBSD	freebsd
HP-UX	hpux
IRIX	irix
Linux	linux
MacOS X	macosx
NetBSD	netbsd
OpenBSD	openbsd
Solaris	solaris

Table 2.2: Processor Architecture Abbreviations

Processor(s)	Abbreviation
Compaq Alpha	alpha
HP Precision Architecture	hppa
INTEL 80x86	intel
INTEL 80x86 w/64bit Extensions	x86_64
MIPS RISC	mips
IBM Power PC	powerpc
SPARC MicroSPARC UltraSPARC	sparc

The `architecture` string identifies the target processor. Table 2.2 lists the supported processors.

Once you have determined the subdirectory containing the distribution, type the following commands to install EPM from the portable distribution:

```
cd os-major.minor-architecture ENTER
./epm.install ENTER
```

The software will be installed after answering a few yes/no questions.

Installing Using the Native Distribution

The `test` target also builds a distribution in the native operating system format, if supported. Table 2.3 lists the native formats for each supported operating system and the command to run to install the software.

Table 2.3: Native Operating System Formats

Operating System	Format	Command
AIX	aix	`installp -d`*directory* `epm`
Compaq Tru64 UNIX Digital UNIX OSF/1	setld	`setld -a` *directory*
FreeBSD NetBSD OpenBSD	bsd	`cd` *directory* `pkg_add epm`
HP-UX	depot	`swinstall -f` *directory*
IRIX	inst	`swmgr -f` *directory*
Linux	rpm	`rpm -i` *directory*`/epm-4.1.rpm`
MacOS X	osx	`open` *directory*`/epm-4.1.pkg`
Solaris	pkg	`pkgadd -d` *directory* `epm`

3 - Packaging Your Software with EPM

This chapter describes how to use EPM to package your own software packages.

The Basics

EPM reads one or more software "list" files that describe a single software package. Each list file contains one or more lines of ASCII text containing product or file information.

Comments lines start with the # character, directive lines start with the % character, variables lines start with the $ character, and file, directory, init script, and symlink lines start with a letter.

Product Information

Every list file needs to define the product name, copyright, description, license, README file, vendor, and version:

```
%product Kung Foo Firewall
%copyright 1999-2005 by Foo Industries, All Rights Reserved.
%vendor Foo Industries
%license COPYING
%readme README
%description Kung Foo firewall software for your firewall.
%version 1.2.3p4 1020304
```

The `%license` and `%readme` directives specify files for the license agreement and README files for the package, respectively.

The `%product`, `%copyright`, `%vendor`, and `%description` directives take text directly from the line.

The `%version` directive specifies the version numbers of the package. The first number is the human-readable version number, while the second number is the integer version number. If you omit the integer version number, EPM will calculate one for you.

Files, Directories, and Symlinks

Each file in the distribution is listed on a line starting with a letter. The format of all lines is:

```
type mode owner group destination source options
```

Regular files use the letter f for the type field:

```
f 755 root sys /usr/bin/foo foo
```

Configuration files use the letter c for the type field:

```
c 644 root sys /etc/foo.conf foo.conf
```

Directories use the letter d for the type field and use a source path of "-":

```
d 755 root sys /var/spool/foo -
```

Finally, symbolic links use the letter l (lowercase L) for the type field:

```
l 000 root sys /usr/bin/foobar foo
```

The source field specifies the file to link to and can be a relative path.

Wildcards

Wildcard patterns can be used in the source field to include multiple files on a single line:

```
f 0444 root sys /usr/share/doc/foo *.html
```

Subpackages

Subpackages are optional parts of your software package. For example, if your package includes developer files, you might provide them as a subpackage so that users that will not be developing add-ons to your software can omit them from the installation.

> **Note:**
> Subpackages are implemented as native subsets of the main package for the AIX, HPUX, IRIX, Solaris, and Tru64 formats and as separate packages that depend on the main (parent) package for all other formats.

To define a subpackage, use the %subpackage directive followed by a %description directive:

```
%subpackage foo
%description One-Line Description of Foo
```

Files, scripts, and dependencies that follow the %subpackage directive are treated as part of that subpackage. Specifying the %subpackage directive with no name returns processing to the main (parent) package.

You can alternate between subpackages as many times as you like:

```
%description Main package description
f 0755 /usr/bin/bar bar

%subpackage foo
%description Foo programs
f 0755 /usr/bin/foo foo
%requires bla

%subpackage
f 0644 /usr/share/man/man1/bar.1

%subpackage foo
f 0644 /usr/share/man/man1/foo.1
```

The above example creates a package containing the "bar" program and man page with a subpackage containing the "foo" program and man page. The "foo" subpackage depends both on the main package (implicit %requires) and another package called "bla".

Building a Software Package

The epm(1) program is used to build software package from list files. To build a portable software package for an application called "foo", type the following command:

```
epm foo ENTER
```

If your application uses a different base name than the list file, you can specify the list filename on the command-line as well:

```
epm foo bar.list ENTER
```

Figure 3.1: The EPM Setup GUI

Installing the Software Package

Once you have created the software package, you can install it. Portable packages include an installation script called *product.install*, where "product" is the name of the package:

```
cd os-release-arch ENTER
./product.install ENTER
```

After answering a few yes/no questions, the software will be installed. To bypass the questions, run the script with the now argument:

```
cd os-release-arch ENTER
./product.install now ENTER
```

Including the Setup GUI

EPM also provides an optional graphical setup program (Figure 3.1). To include the setup program in your distributions, create a product logo image in GIF or XPM format and use the `--setup-image` option when creating your distribution:

```
epm --setup-image foo.xpm foo ENTER
```

This option is only supported when creating for portable and MacOS X software packages.

Creating Vendor Package Files

EPM can also produce vendor-specific packages using the `-f` option:

```
epm -f format foo bar.list ENTER
```

The *format* option can be one of the following keywords:

- `aix` - AIX software packages.
- `bsd` - FreeBSD, NetBSD, or OpenBSD software packages.
- `depot` or `swinstall` - HP-UX software packages.
- `dpkg` - Debian software packages.
- `inst` or `tardist` - IRIX software packages.
- `native` - "Native" software packages (RPM, INST, DEPOT, PKG, etc.) for the platform.
- `osx` - MacOS X software packages.
- `pkg` - Solaris software packages.
- `portable` - Portable software packages (default).
- `rpm` - Red Hat software packages.
- `setld` - Tru64 (setld) software packages.
- `slackware` - Slackware software packages.

Everything in the software list file stays the same - you just use the `-f` option to select the format. For example, to build an RPM distribution of EPM, type:

```
epm -f rpm epm
```

The result will be one or more RPM package files instead of the portable package files.

Package Files

EPM creates the package files in the output directory. As mentioned in Chapter 1, "Installing Using the Portable Distribution", the default output directory is based on the operating system name, version, and architecture. Each package format will leave different files in the output directory.

AIX Package Files

AIX packages are contained in a file called *name.bff*, where "name" is the product/package name you supplied on the command-line.

BSD Package Files

BSD packages are contained in a file called *name.tgz*, where "name" is the product/package name you supplied on the command-line.

HP-UX Package Files

HP-UX packages are contained in two files called *name.depot.gz* and *name.depot.tgz*, where "name" is the product/package name you supplied on the command-line. The *name.depot.gz* file can be supplied directly to the swinstall(1m) command, while the *name.depot.tgz* file contains a compressed tar(1) archive that can be used to install the software from CD-ROM or network filesystem.

Debian Package Files

Debian packages are contained in a file called *name.deb* or *name.deb.tgz* when there are subpackages, where "name" is the product/package name you supplied on the command-line. The *name.deb.tgz* file contains a compressed tar archive containing *name.deb* and *name-subpackage.deb* files that can be installed from CD-ROM, disk, or network filesystem.

IRIX Package Files

IRIX packages are contained in a file called *name.tardist*, where "name" is the product/package name you supplied on the command-line.

MacOS X Package Files

MacOS X packages are contained in a file called *name.dmg*, where "name" is the product/package name you supplied on the command-line.

RPM Package Files

RPM packages are contained in a file called *name.rpm* or *name.rpm.tgz* when there are subpackages, where "name" is the product/package name you supplied on the command-line. The *name.rpm.tgz* file contains a compressed `tar` archive containing *name.rpm* and *name-subpackage.rpm* files that can be installed from CD-ROM, disk, or network filesystem.

Slackware Package Files

Slackware packages are contained in a file called *name.tgz*, where "name" is the product/package name you supplied on the command-line.

Solaris Package Files

Solaris packages are contained in two files called *name.pkg.gz* and *name.pkg.tgz*, where "name" is the product/package name you supplied on the command-line. The *name.pkg.gz* file is a compressed package file that can be used directly with the `pkgadd(1m)` command, while the *name.pkg.tgz* file is a compressed `tar` archive that can be used to install the software from CD-ROM, disk, or network filesystem.

Tru64 Package Files

Tru64 packages are contained in a file called *name.tar.gz*, where "name" is the product/package name you supplied on the command-line.

4 - Advanced Packaging with EPM

This chapter describes the advanced packaging features of EPM.

Including Other List Files

The `%include` directive includes another list file:

```
%include filename
```

Includes can usually be nested up to 250 levels depending on the host operating system and libraries.

Dependencies

EPM supports four types of dependencies in list files: `%incompat`, `%provides`, `%replaces`, and `%requires`. Table 4.1 shows the level of support for each package format.

Table 4.1: Dependency Support

Format	%incompat	%provides	%replaces	%requires
aix	No	No	Yes	Yes
bsd	Yes	No	No	Yes
deb	Yes	Yes[1]	Yes	Yes
inst	Yes	No	Yes	Yes
osx	No	No	No	No
pkg	Yes	No	No	Yes
portable	Yes	Yes	Yes	Yes
rpm	Yes	Yes	No	Yes
setld	No	No	No	No
slackware	No	No	No	No
swinstall	No	No	Yes	Yes

1. Debian's package format does not currently support version numbers for %provides dependencies.

Software conflicts and requirements are specified using the %incompat and %requires directives.

If your software replaces another package, you can specify that using the %replaces directive. %replaces is silently mapped to %incompat when the package format does not support package replacement.

If your package provides certain functionality associated with a standard name, the %provides directive can be used.

Dependencies are specified using the package name and optionally the lower and upper version numbers:

```
%requires foobar
%requires foobar 1.0
%incompat foobar 0.9
%replaces foobar
%replaces foobar 1.2 3.4
%provides foobar
```

or the filename:

```
%requires /usr/lib/libfoobar.so
%incompat /usr/lib/libfoobar.so.1.2
```

Package dependencies are currently enforced only for the same package format, so a portable distribution that requires package "foobar" will only look for an installed "foobar" package in portable format.

Filename dependencies are only supported by the Debian, portable, and RPM distribution formats.

Scripts

Bourne shell script commands can be executed before or after installation, patching, or removal of the software. Table 4.2 shows the support for scripts in each package format.

The %preinstall and %postinstall directives specify commands to be run before and after installation, respectively:

```
%preinstall echo Command before installing
%postinstall echo Command after installing
```

Similarly, the %prepatch and %postpatch directives specify commands to be executed before and after patching the software:

```
%prepatch echo Command before patching
%postpatch echo Command after patching
```

Finally, the %preremove and %postremove directives specify commands that are run before and after removal of the software:

```
%preremove echo Command before removing
%postremove echo Command after removing
```

Table 4.2: Scripts Support

Format	%preinstall	%postinstall	%prepatch	%postpatch	%preremove	%postremove
aix	Yes	Yes	No	No	Yes	Yes
bsd	No	Yes	No	No	Yes	No
deb	Yes	Yes	No	No	Yes	Yes
inst	Yes	Yes	No	No	Yes	Yes
osx	Yes	Yes	No	No	No	No
pkg	Yes	Yes	No	No	Yes	Yes
portable	Yes	Yes	Yes	Yes	Yes	Yes
rpm	Yes	Yes	No	No	Yes	Yes
setld	Yes	Yes	No	No	Yes	Yes
slackware	No	Yes	No	No	No	No
swinstall	Yes	Yes	No	No	Yes	Yes

To include an external script file, use the `<filename` notation:

```
%postinstall <filename
```

To include multiple lines directly, use the `<<string` notation (a.k.a. a "here" document):

```
%postinstall <<EOF
echo Command before installing
/usr/bin/foo
EOF
```

Note that all commands specified in the list file will use the variable expansion provided by EPM, so be sure to quote any dollar sign ($) characters in your commands. For example, "$foo" is replaced by the value of "foo", but "$$foo" becomes "$foo".

Conditional Directives

The %system directive can match or not match specific operating system names or versions. The operating system name is the name reported by uname in lowercase, while the operating system version is the major and minor version number reported by uname -r:

```
%system irix
```

> Only include the following files when building a distribution for the IRIX operating system.

```
%system linux-2.0
```

> Only include the following files when building a distribution for Linux 2.0.x.

```
%system !irix !linux-2.0
```

> Only include the following files when building a distribution for operating systems other than IRIX and Linux 2.0.x.

The special name all is used to match all operating systems:

```
%system all
```

For format-specific files, the %format directive can be used:

```
%format rpm
```

> Only include the following files when building an RPM distribution.

```
%format !rpm
```

> Only include the following files when not building an RPM distribution.x.

```
%format all
```

>   Include the following files for all types of
>   distributions.

The %arch directive can match or not match specific
architectures. The architecture name is the name reported
by uname -m; "arm" is a synonym for "armv6", "armv7", and
"armv8", "intel" is a synonym for "i386", "i486", "i586", and
"i686", and "powerpc" is a synonym for "ppc":

```
%arch intel
```

>   Only include the following files when building
>   a package for 32-bit Intel processors.

```
%arch armv6
```

>   Only include the following files when building
>   a package for ARMv6 processors.

```
%system !powerpc
```

>   Only include the following files when building
>   a package for processors other than PowerPC.

The special name all is used to match all architectures:

```
%arch all
```

Finally, EPM can conditionally include lines using the %if,
%elseif, %ifdef, %elseifdef, %else, and %endif directives.

%if directives include the text that follows if the named
variable(s) are defined to a non-empty string:

```
%if FOO
f 755 root sys /usr/bin/foo foo
%elseif BAR
```

```
f 755 root sys /usr/bin/bar bar
%endif
```

`%ifdef` directives only include the text if the named variable(s) are defined to any value:

```
%ifdef OSTYPE
f 755 root sys /usr/bin/program program-$OSTYPE
%else
f 755 root sys /usr/bin/program program.sh
%endif
```

Protecting Object Files from Stripping

The `nostrip()` option can be included at the end of a file line to prevent EPM from stripping the symbols and debugging information from a file:

```
f 755 root sys /usr/lib/libfoo.so libfoo.so nostrip()
```

Software Patches

EPM supports portable software patch distributions which contain only the differences between the original and patch release. Patch files are specified using uppercase letters for the affected files. In the following example, the files */usr/bin/bar* and */etc/foo.conf* are marked

as changed since the original release:

```
f 755 root sys /usr/bin/foo foo
F 755 root sys /usr/bin/bar bar
f 755 root sys /usr/share/man/man1/foo.1 foo.man
f 755 root sys /usr/share/man/man1/bar.1 bar.man
C 644 root sys /etc/foo.conf foo.conf
```

Variables

EPM imports the current environment variables for use in your list file. You can also define new variable in the list file or on the command-line when running EPM.

Variables are defined by starting the line with the dollar sign ($) followed by the name and value:

```
$name=value
$prefix=/usr
$exec_prefix=${prefix}
$bindir=$exec_prefix/bin
```

Variable substitution is performed when the variable is defined, so be careful with the ordering of your variable definitions.

Also, any variables you specify in your list file will be overridden by variables defined on the command-line or in your environment, just like with make. This can be a useful feature or a curse, depending on your choice of variable names.

As you can see, variables are referenced using the dollar sign ($). As with most shells, variable names can be surrounded by curly braces (${variable}) to explicitly delimit the name.

If you need to insert a $ in a filename or a script, use $$:

```
%install echo Enter your name:
%install read $$name
%install echo Your name is $$name.
```

Init Scripts

Initialization scripts are generally portable between platforms, however the location of initialization scripts varies greatly.

The i file type can be used to specify and init script that is to be installed on the system. EPM will then determine the appropriate init file directories to use and create any required symbolic links to support the init script:

```
i 755 root sys foo foo.sh
```

The previous example creates an init script named *foo* on the end-user system and will create symbolic links to run levels 0, 2, 3, and 5 as needed, using a sequence number of 00 (or 000) for the shutdown script and 99 (or 999) for the startup script.

To specify run levels and sequence numbers, use the `runlevel()`, `start()`, and `stop()` options:

```
i 755 root sys foo foo.sh "runlevel(02) start(50) stop(30)"
```

Literal Package Data

Sometimes you need to include format-specific package data such as keywords, signing keys, and response data. The `%literal(section)` directive adds format-specific data to the packages you create. Literal data is currently only supported for RPM and PKG packages.

PKG Literal Data

PKG packages support request files that are used to do batch installations when installation commands require user input. The `%literal(request)` directive can be used to provide this user input:

```
%literal(request) <<EOF
John Doe
1 Any Lane
Forest Lawn, OH 12345
EOF
```

RPM Literal Data

RPM packages support numerous attributes in the "spec" file that control how the package is created and what metadata is included with the package. The `%literal(spec)` directive can be used to provide attributes for the spec file:

```
%literal(spec) <<EOF
%changelog
* Tue Aug 26 2008 John Doe <johndoe@domain.com>
```

- Added new feature "bar"

* Fri Aug 1 2008 John Doe <johndoe@domain.com>

- Added new feature "foo"
EOF

5 - EPM Packaging Examples

This chapter shows how the EPM and CUPS software is packaged using EPM list files. The EPM list file example highlights the basic features of EPM, while the CUPS list file example shows the more advanced features of EPM.

Packaging the EPM Software

The EPM software comes with its own autoconf-generated *epm.list* file that is used to package and test EPM. The EPM package consists of the main package plus a "documentation" subpackage for the documentation files and a "man" subpackage for the man pages.

We start by defining variables for each of the autoconf directory variables:

```
$prefix=/usr
$exec_prefix=/usr
$bindir=${exec_prefix}/bin
$datadir=/usr/share
$docdir=${datadir}/doc/epm
```

```
$libdir=/usr/lib
$mandir=/usr/share/man
$srcdir=.
```

Then we provide the general product information that is required for all packages; notice the use of ${srcdir} to reference the COPYING and README files:

```
%product ESP Package Manager
%copyright 1999-2006 by Easy Software Products, All Rights Reserved.
%vendor Easy Software Products
%license ${srcdir}/COPYING
%readme ${srcdir}/README
%description Universal software packaging tool for UNIX.
%version 4.0 400
```

After the product information, we include all of the non-GUI files that are part of EPM:

```
# Executables
%system all
f 0555 root sys ${bindir}/epm epm
f 0555 root sys ${bindir}/epminstall epminstall
f 0555 root sys ${bindir}/mkepmlist mkepmlist

# Documentation
%subpackage documentation
%description Documentation for EPM
f 0444 root sys ${docdir}/README $srcdir/README
f 0444 root sys ${docdir}/COPYING $srcdir/COPYING
f 0444 root sys ${docdir}/epm-book.html $srcdir/doc/epm-book.html

# Man pages
%subpackage man
%description Man pages for EPM
f 0444 root sys ${mandir}/man1/epm.1 $srcdir/doc/epm.man
f 0444 root sys ${mandir}/man1/epminstall.1 $srcdir/doc/epminstall.man
f 0444 root sys ${mandir}/man1/mkepmlist.1 $srcdir/doc/mkepmlist.man
f 0444 root sys ${mandir}/man5/epm.list.5 $srcdir/doc/epm.list.man
```

Finally, we conditionally include the GUI files depending on the state of a variable called GUIS:

```
# GUI files...
$GUIS=setup uninst

%if GUIS
%subpackage
f 0555 root sys ${libdir}/epm/setup setup
f 0555 root sys ${libdir}/epm/uninst uninst

%system darwin
f 0444 root sys ${datadir}/epm/setup.icns macosx/setup.icns
```

```
f 0444 root sys ${datadir}/epm/setup.info macosx/setup.info
f 0444 root sys ${datadir}/epm/setup.plist macosx/setup.plist

f 0444 root sys ${datadir}/epm/uninst.icns macosx/uninst.icns
f 0444 root sys ${datadir}/epm/uninst.info macosx/uninst.info
f 0444 root sys ${datadir}/epm/uninst.plist macosx/uninst.plist
%system all

%subpackage man
f 0444 root sys ${mandir}/man1/setup.1 $srcdir/doc/setup.man
f 0444 root sys ${mandir}/man5/setup.types.5 $srcdir/doc/setup.types.man

%endif
```

Packaging the CUPS Software

The Common UNIX Printing System provides an EPM list file to generate software distributions for most UNIX operating systems. This list file is more complex than the EPM example and contains several subpackages:

- "devel"; Developer header, library, and documentation files
- "es"; Spanish localization files
- "ja"; Japanese localization files
- "libs"; Shared libraries
- "lpd"; LPD client support

Variables Used for the Distribution

In addition to the autoconf variables defined in the EPM list file, the CUPS list file defines the following autoconf-derived variables for the distribution:

- AMANDIR; The directory for administrative manual pages.
- BINDIR; The directory for user programs.
- CACHEDIR; The directory for cache files.
- DATADIR; The directory for data files.
- DOCDIR; The directory for documentation files.
- INCLUDEDIR; The directory for header files.
- INITDIR; The directory for startup scripts.
- INITDDIR; The directory to reference from run-level scripts.
- LIBDIR; The directory for library files.

- `LIB32DIR`; The directory for 32-bit library files.
- `LIB64DIR`; The directory for 64-bit library files.
- `LOCALEDIR`; The directory for message (localization) files.
- `LOGDIR`; The directory for log files.
- `MANDIR`; The directory for man pages.
- `PAMDIR`; The directory for PAM configuration files.
- `REQUESTS`; The directory for request files.
- `SBINDIR`; The directory for administration programs.
- `SERVERBIN`; The directory for server programs.
- `SERVERROOT`; The directory for server configuration files.
- `STATEDIR`; The directory for server state files.

Product Information

The list file starts with the standard product information:

```
%product Common UNIX Printing System
%copyright 1993-2006 by Easy Software Products, All Rights Reserved.
%vendor Easy Software Products
%license LICENSE.txt
%readme packaging/cups.license
%version 1.2.0
%description The Common UNIX Printing System provides a portable
%description printing layer for UNIX(r) operating systems.  It
%description has been developed by Easy Software Products to
%description promote a standard printing solution for all UNIX
%description vendors and users.  CUPS provides the System V and
%description Berkeley command-line interfaces.
```

We then list different dependencies depending on the package format:

```
%format rpm
%provides cups 1:1.2.0
%provides lpd, lpr, LPRng
%replaces lpd, lpr, LPRng

%format deb
%provides cupsys
%provides cupsys-client
%provides cupsys-bsd

%format pkg
%replaces SUNWlpmsg LP Alerts
%replaces SUNWlpr LP Print Service, (Root)
%replaces SUNWlps LP Print Service - Server, (Usr)
%replaces SUNWlpu LP Print Service - Client, (Usr)
```

```
%replaces SUNWpsu LP Print Server, (Usr)
%replaces SUNWpsr LP Print Server, (Root)
%replaces SUNWpcu LP Print Client, (Usr)
%replaces SUNWpcr LP Print Client, (Root)
%replaces SUNWppm
%replaces SUNWmp
%replaces SUNWscplp SunOS Print Compatibility

%format inst
%replaces patch*.print_*.* 0 0 1289999999 1289999999
%replaces maint*.print_*.* 0 0 1289999999 1289999999
%replaces print 0 0 1289999999 1289999999
%replaces fw_cups 0 0 1289999999 1289999999
%incompat patch*.print_*.* 0 0 1289999999 1289999999
%incompat maint*.print_*.* 0 0 1289999999 1289999999
%incompat print 0 0 1289999999 1289999999
%incompat fw_cups 0 0 1289999999 1289999999

%format all
```

The subpackages come next, each with their own dependencies:

```
%subpackage libs
%description Common UNIX Printing System - shared libraries
%format rpm
%provides cups-libs 1:1.2.0
%format deb
%provides libcups1
%provides libcupsys2
%provides libcupsys2-gnutls10
%provides libcupsimage2
%format all

%subpackage devel
%description Common UNIX Printing System - development environment
%format rpm
%provides cups-devel 1:1.2.0
%format deb
%provides libcupsys2-dev
%provides libcupsimage2-dev
%format all

%subpackage lpd
%description Common UNIX Printing System - LPD support
%format rpm
%provides cups-lpd 1:1.2.0
%format all

%subpackage es
%description Common UNIX Printing System - Spanish support

%subpackage ja
%description Common UNIX Printing System - Japanese support

%subpackage
```

Server Programs

The server programs are installed in the SBINDIR and
SERVERBIN directories. The image and PDF filters are
conditionally included based on the IMGFILTERS and PDFTOPS
variables, respectively:

```
f 0755 root sys $SBINDIR/cupsd scheduler/cupsd

d 0755 root sys $SERVERBIN -
d 0755 root sys $SERVERBIN/backend -
f 0755 root sys $SERVERBIN/backend/ipp backend/ipp
l 0755 root sys $SERVERBIN/backend/http ipp
f 0755 root sys $SERVERBIN/backend/lpd backend/lpd
f 0755 root sys $SERVERBIN/backend/parallel backend/parallel
f 0755 root sys $SERVERBIN/backend/scsi backend/scsi
f 0755 root sys $SERVERBIN/backend/serial backend/serial
f 0755 root sys $SERVERBIN/backend/socket backend/socket
f 0755 root sys $SERVERBIN/backend/usb backend/usb
d 0755 root sys $SERVERBIN/cgi-bin -
f 0755 root sys $SERVERBIN/cgi-bin/admin.cgi cgi-bin/admin.cgi
f 0755 root sys $SERVERBIN/cgi-bin/classes.cgi cgi-bin/classes.cgi
f 0755 root sys $SERVERBIN/cgi-bin/help.cgi cgi-bin/help.cgi
f 0755 root sys $SERVERBIN/cgi-bin/jobs.cgi cgi-bin/jobs.cgi
f 0755 root sys $SERVERBIN/cgi-bin/printers.cgi cgi-bin/printers.cgi
d 0755 root sys $SERVERBIN/daemon -
f 0755 root sys $SERVERBIN/daemon/cups-deviced scheduler/cups-deviced
f 0755 root sys $SERVERBIN/daemon/cups-driverd scheduler/cups-driverd
f 0755 root sys $SERVERBIN/daemon/cups-polld scheduler/cups-polld
d 0755 root sys $SERVERBIN/driver -
d 0755 root sys $SERVERBIN/filter -
f 0755 root sys $SERVERBIN/filter/gziptoany filter/gziptoany
f 0755 root sys $SERVERBIN/filter/hpgltops filter/hpgltops
%if IMGFILTERS
f 0755 root sys $SERVERBIN/filter/imagetops filter/imagetops
f 0755 root sys $SERVERBIN/filter/imagetoraster filter/imagetoraster
%endif
%if PDFTOPS
f 0755 root sys $SERVERBIN/filter/pdftops pdftops/pdftops
%endif
f 0755 root sys $SERVERBIN/filter/pstops filter/pstops
f 0755 root sys $SERVERBIN/filter/rastertolabel filter/rastertolabel
l 0755 root sys $SERVERBIN/filter/rastertodymo rastertolabel
f 0755 root sys $SERVERBIN/filter/rastertoepson filter/rastertoepson
f 0755 root sys $SERVERBIN/filter/rastertohp filter/rastertohp
f 0755 root sys $SERVERBIN/filter/texttops filter/texttops
d 0755 root sys $SERVERBIN/notifier -
f 0755 root sys $SERVERBIN/notifier/mailto notifier/mailto
```

The cups-lpd program goes in the "lpd" subpackage:

```
%subpackage lpd
d 0755 root sys $SERVERBIN/daemon -
f 0755 root sys $SERVERBIN/daemon/cups-lpd scheduler/cups-lpd
```

%subpackage

Administration Commands

The administration commands are all pretty much the same.
The only difference is that IRIX needs a symlink for the `lpc`
program in the */usr/etc* directory.

```
d 0755 root sys $BINDIR -
l 0755 root sys $BINDIR/enable $SBINDIR/accept
l 0755 root sys $LIBDIR/accept $SBINDIR/accept
d 0755 root sys $SBINDIR -
l 0755 root sys $SBINDIR/cupsdisable accept
l 0755 root sys $SBINDIR/cupsenable accept
l 0755 root sys $BINDIR/disable $SBINDIR/accept
d 0755 root sys $LIBDIR -
l 0755 root sys $LIBDIR/lpadmin $SBINDIR/lpadmin
l 0755 root sys $LIBDIR/reject accept
f 0755 root sys $SBINDIR/accept systemv/accept
f 0755 root sys $SBINDIR/cupsaddsmb systemv/cupsaddsmb
f 0755 root sys $SBINDIR/lpadmin systemv/lpadmin
f 0755 root sys $SBINDIR/lpc berkeley/lpc
f 0755 root sys $SBINDIR/lpinfo systemv/lpinfo
f 0755 root sys $SBINDIR/lpmove systemv/lpmove
l 0755 root sys $SBINDIR/reject accept

%system irix
l 0755 root sys /usr/etc/lpc $SBINDIR/lpc
%system all
```

User Commands

The user commands are all pretty much the same. As with
the administration commands, IRIX needs the Berkeley
commands linked to a different directory, */usr/bsd*.

```
d 0755 root sys $BINDIR -
f 0755 root sys $BINDIR/cancel systemv/cancel
f 0755 root sys $BINDIR/cupstestdsc systemv/cupstestdsc
f 0755 root sys $BINDIR/cupstestppd systemv/cupstestppd
f 0755 root sys $BINDIR/lp systemv/lp
f 0755 root sys $BINDIR/lpoptions systemv/lpoptions
f 4755 $CUPS_USER sys $BINDIR/lppasswd systemv/lppasswd
f 0755 root sys $BINDIR/lpq berkeley/lpq
f 0755 root sys $BINDIR/lpr berkeley/lpr
f 0755 root sys $BINDIR/lprm berkeley/lprm
f 0755 root sys $BINDIR/lpstat systemv/lpstat

%system irix
l 0755 root sys /usr/bsd/lpq $BINDIR/lpq
l 0755 root sys /usr/bsd/lpr $BINDIR/lpr
l 0755 root sys /usr/bsd/lprm $BINDIR/lprm
```

```
%system all
```

Shared Libraries

Shared libraries present their own challenges. AIX, HP-UX, and MacOS X uses a different extension for shared libraries than the other operating systems, and we only include the shared libraries if they are enabled in the build:

```
%if DSOLIBS
%subpackage libs
%system hpux
f 0755 root sys $LIBDIR/libcups.sl.2 cups/libcups.sl.2
l 0755 root sys $LIBDIR/libcups.sl libcups.sl.2
f 0755 root sys $LIBDIR/libcupsimage.sl.2 filter/libcupsimage.sl.2
l 0755 root sys $LIBDIR/libcupsimage.sl libcupsimage.sl.2
%system aix
f 0755 root sys $LIBDIR/libcups_s.a cups/libcups_s.a
f 0755 root sys $LIBDIR/libcupsimage_s.a filter/libcupsimage_s.a
%system darwin
f 0755 root sys $LIBDIR/libcups.2.dylib cups/libcups.2.dylib
l 0755 root sys $LIBDIR/libcups.dylib libcups.2.dylib
f 0755 root sys $LIBDIR/libcupsimage.2.dylib filter/libcupsimage.2.dylib
l 0755 root sys $LIBDIR/libcupsimage.dylib libcupsimage.2.dylib
%system !hpux !aix !darwin
f 0755 root sys $LIBDIR/libcups.so.2 cups/libcups.so.2
l 0755 root sys $LIBDIR/libcups.so libcups.so.2
f 0755 root sys $LIBDIR/libcupsimage.so.2 filter/libcupsimage.so.2
l 0755 root sys $LIBDIR/libcupsimage.so libcupsimage.so.2
%system all
%subpackage
%endif
```

To keep things interesting, CUPS also supports separately compiled 32-bit and 64-bit libraries on systems that support a mix of 32-bit and 64-bit binaries. The LIB32DIR and LIB64DIR variables are used to conditionally include the corresponding libraries:

```
%if LIB32DIR
%subpackage libs
f 0755 root sys $LIB32DIR/libcups.so.2 cups/libcups.32.so.2
l 0755 root sys $LIB32DIR/libcups.so libcups.so.2
f 0755 root sys $LIB32DIR/libcupsimage.so.2 filter/libcupsimage.32.so.2
l 0755 root sys $LIB32DIR/libcupsimage.so libcupsimage.so.2
%system all
%subpackage
%endif

%if LIB64DIR
%subpackage libs
f 0755 root sys $LIB64DIR/libcups.so.2 cups/libcups.64.so.2
```

```
l 0755 root sys $LIB64DIR/libcups.so libcups.so.2
f 0755 root sys $LIB64DIR/libcupsimage.so.2 filter/libcupsimage.64.so.2
l 0755 root sys $LIB64DIR/libcupsimage.so libcupsimage.so.2
%system all
%subpackage
%endif
```

Directories

The CUPS distribution uses several directories to hold the log, request, and temporary files. The CUPS_GROUP and CUPS_PRIMARY_SYSTEM_GROUP variables define the group names to use for these directories:

```
d 0755 root sys $LOGDIR -
d 0710 root $CUPS_GROUP $REQUESTS -
d 1770 root $CUPS_GROUP $REQUESTS/tmp -
d 0775 root $CUPS_GROUP $CACHEDIR -
d 0755 root $CUPS_GROUP $STATEDIR -
d 0511 root $CUPS_PRIMARY_SYSTEM_GROUP $STATEDIR/certs -
```

Data Files

CUPS has lots of data files. We use wildcards whenever possible:

```
d 0755 root sys $DATADIR -

d 0755 root sys $DATADIR/banners -
f 0644 root sys $DATADIR/banners/classified data/classified
f 0644 root sys $DATADIR/banners/confidential data/confidential
f 0644 root sys $DATADIR/banners/secret data/secret
f 0644 root sys $DATADIR/banners/standard data/standard
f 0644 root sys $DATADIR/banners/topsecret data/topsecret
f 0644 root sys $DATADIR/banners/unclassified data/unclassified

d 0755 root sys $DATADIR/charsets -
f 0644 root sys $DATADIR/charsets data/*.txt
f 0644 root sys $DATADIR/charsets/windows-874 data/windows-874
f 0644 root sys $DATADIR/charsets/windows-1250 data/windows-1250
f 0644 root sys $DATADIR/charsets/windows-1251 data/windows-1251
f 0644 root sys $DATADIR/charsets/windows-1252 data/windows-1252
f 0644 root sys $DATADIR/charsets/windows-1253 data/windows-1253
f 0644 root sys $DATADIR/charsets/windows-1254 data/windows-1254
f 0644 root sys $DATADIR/charsets/windows-1255 data/windows-1255
f 0644 root sys $DATADIR/charsets/windows-1256 data/windows-1256
f 0644 root sys $DATADIR/charsets/windows-1257 data/windows-1257
f 0644 root sys $DATADIR/charsets/windows-1258 data/windows-1258
f 0644 root sys $DATADIR/charsets/iso-8859-1 data/iso-8859-1
f 0644 root sys $DATADIR/charsets/iso-8859-2 data/iso-8859-2
f 0644 root sys $DATADIR/charsets/iso-8859-3 data/iso-8859-3
f 0644 root sys $DATADIR/charsets/iso-8859-4 data/iso-8859-4
```

```
f 0644 root sys $DATADIR/charsets/iso-8859-5 data/iso-8859-5
f 0644 root sys $DATADIR/charsets/iso-8859-6 data/iso-8859-6
f 0644 root sys $DATADIR/charsets/iso-8859-7 data/iso-8859-7
f 0644 root sys $DATADIR/charsets/iso-8859-8 data/iso-8859-8
f 0644 root sys $DATADIR/charsets/iso-8859-9 data/iso-8859-9
f 0644 root sys $DATADIR/charsets/iso-8859-10 data/iso-8859-10
f 0644 root sys $DATADIR/charsets/iso-8859-13 data/iso-8859-13
f 0644 root sys $DATADIR/charsets/iso-8859-14 data/iso-8859-14
f 0644 root sys $DATADIR/charsets/iso-8859-15 data/iso-8859-15
f 0644 root sys $DATADIR/charsets/utf-8 data/utf-8

d 0755 root sys $DATADIR/data -
f 0644 root sys $DATADIR/data/HPGLprolog data/HPGLprolog
f 0644 root sys $DATADIR/data/psglyphs data/psglyphs
f 0644 root sys $DATADIR/data/testprint.ps data/testprint.ps

d 0755 root sys $DATADIR/fonts -
f 0644 root sys $DATADIR/fonts fonts/Courier*
f 0644 root sys $DATADIR/fonts/Symbol fonts/Symbol

d 0755 root sys $DATADIR/model -
f 0644 root sys $DATADIR/model ppd/*.ppd

d 0755 root sys $DATADIR/templates -
c 0644 root sys $DATADIR/templates templates/*.tmpl
```

The template files for each of the language localizations are put in separate subpackages:

```
# Japanese template files
%subpackage es
d 0755 root sys $DATADIR/templates/es -
f 0644 root sys $DATADIR/templates/es templates/es/*.tmpl
%subpackage ja
d 0755 root sys $DATADIR/templates/ja -
f 0644 root sys $DATADIR/templates/ja templates/ja/*.tmpl
%subpackage
```

Configuration Files

The server configuration files and directories go in SERVERROOT. The MIME configuration files are not treated as configuration files in the distribution since new versions of CUPS may add filters and file types that are required to make CUPS work:

```
d 0755 root sys $SERVERROOT -
d 0755 root $CUPS_GROUP $SERVERROOT/interfaces -
d 0755 root $CUPS_GROUP $SERVERROOT/ppd -
c $CUPS_PERM root $CUPS_GROUP $SERVERROOT conf/*.conf
f $CUPS_PERM root $CUPS_GROUP $SERVERROOT/cupsd.conf.default conf/cupsd.conf
f $CUPS_PERM root $CUPS_GROUP $SERVERROOT/mime.convs conf/mime.convs
f $CUPS_PERM root $CUPS_GROUP $SERVERROOT/mime.types conf/mime.types
```

The PAM configuration file is only included if the configure script found a PAM configuration directory:

```
%if PAMDIR
d 0755 root sys $PAMDIR -
c 0644 root sys $PAMDIR/cups conf/pam.std
%endif
```

Developer Files

The developer files include the C header files, static libraries, and help files. The static libraries are only included if they have been built, which is specified using the INSTALLSTATIC variable:

```
%subpackage devel
f 0755 root sys $BINDIR/cups-config cups-config
d 0755 root sys $INCLUDEDIR/cups -
f 0644 root sys $INCLUDEDIR/cups/cups.h cups/cups.h
f 0644 root sys $INCLUDEDIR/cups/http.h cups/http.h
f 0644 root sys $INCLUDEDIR/cups/image.h filter/image.h
f 0644 root sys $INCLUDEDIR/cups/ipp.h cups/ipp.h
f 0644 root sys $INCLUDEDIR/cups/language.h cups/language.h
f 0644 root sys $INCLUDEDIR/cups/md5.h cups/md5.h
f 0644 root sys $INCLUDEDIR/cups/ppd.h cups/ppd.h
f 0644 root sys $INCLUDEDIR/cups/raster.h filter/raster.h

%if INSTALLSTATIC
f 0644 root sys $LIBDIR/libcups.a cups/libcups.a
f 0644 root sys $LIBDIR/libcupsimage.a filter/libcupsimage.a
%endif

d 0755 root sys $DOCDIR/help -
f 0644 root sys $DOCDIR/help doc/help/api*.html
f 0644 root sys $DOCDIR/help doc/help/spec*.html
%subpackage
```

Documentation Files

The documentation files go under DOCDIR. Wildcards take care of most of the work:

```
d 0755 root sys $DOCDIR -
f 0644 root sys $DOCDIR doc/*.css
f 0644 root sys $DOCDIR doc/*.html
d 0755 root sys $DOCDIR/help -
f 0644 root sys $DOCDIR/help/cgi.html doc/help/cgi.html
f 0644 root sys $DOCDIR/help/glossary.html doc/help/glossary.html
f 0644 root sys $DOCDIR/help/license.html doc/help/license.html
f 0644 root sys $DOCDIR/help/network.html doc/help/network.html
f 0644 root sys $DOCDIR/help/options.html doc/help/options.html
```

```
f 0644 root sys $DOCDIR/help/overview.html doc/help/overview.html
f 0644 root sys $DOCDIR/help/security.html doc/help/security.html
f 0644 root sys $DOCDIR/help/standard.html doc/help/standard.html
f 0644 root sys $DOCDIR/help/translation.html doc/help/translation.html
f 0644 root sys $DOCDIR/help/whatsnew.html doc/help/whatsnew.html
f 0644 root sys $DOCDIR/help doc/help/man-*.html
f 0644 root sys $DOCDIR/help doc/help/ref-*.html
d 0755 root sys $DOCDIR/images -
f 0644 root sys $DOCDIR/images doc/images/*.gif
f 0644 root sys $DOCDIR/images doc/images/*.jpg
f 0644 root sys $DOCDIR/images doc/images/*.png
f 0644 root sys $DOCDIR/robots.txt doc/robots.txt
```

The Japanese and Spanish version of the documentation
files go in the corresponding subpackages:

```
# Localized documentation files
%subpackage es
d 0755 root sys $DOCDIR/es
f 0644 root sys $DOCDIR/es doc/es/*.html
d 0755 root sys $DOCDIR/es/images -
f 0644 root sys $DOCDIR/es/images doc/es/images/*.gif
%subpackage ja
d 0755 root sys $DOCDIR/ja
f 0644 root sys $DOCDIR/ja doc/ja/*.html
d 0755 root sys $DOCDIR/ja/images -
f 0644 root sys $DOCDIR/ja/images doc/ja/images/*.gif
%subpackage
```

Man Pages

Man pages are almost as much fun as initialization scripts.
HP-UX, IRIX, and Solaris follow the System V convention of
using section 1m for administration commands instead of
section 8 as is used for all other operating systems. IRIX also
places administrative commands in a separate subdirectory:

```
d 0755 root sys $AMANDIR -
d 0755 root sys $AMANDIR/man$MAN8DIR -
d 0755 root sys $MANDIR -
d 0755 root sys $MANDIR/man1 -
d 0755 root sys $MANDIR/man5 -
d 0755 root sys $MANDIR/man7 -

f 0644 root sys $MANDIR/man1/cancel.$MAN1EXT man/cancel.$MAN1EXT
f 0644 root sys $MANDIR/man1/cupstestdsc.$MAN1EXT man/cupstestdsc.$MAN1EXT
f 0644 root sys $MANDIR/man1/cupstestppd.$MAN1EXT man/cupstestppd.$MAN1EXT
f 0644 root sys $MANDIR/man1/lpoptions.$MAN1EXT man/lpoptions.$MAN1EXT
f 0644 root sys $MANDIR/man1/lppasswd.$MAN1EXT man/lppasswd.$MAN1EXT
f 0644 root sys $MANDIR/man1/lpq.$MAN1EXT man/lpq.$MAN1EXT
f 0644 root sys $MANDIR/man1/lprm.$MAN1EXT man/lprm.$MAN1EXT
f 0644 root sys $MANDIR/man1/lpr.$MAN1EXT man/lpr.$MAN1EXT
f 0644 root sys $MANDIR/man1/lpstat.$MAN1EXT man/lpstat.$MAN1EXT
```

```
f 0644 root sys $MANDIR/man1/lp.$MAN1EXT man/lp.$MAN1EXT

f 0644 root sys $MANDIR/man5/classes.conf.$MAN5EXT man/classes.conf.$MAN5EXT
f 0644 root sys $MANDIR/man5/cupsd.conf.$MAN5EXT man/cupsd.conf.$MAN5EXT
f 0644 root sys $MANDIR/man5/mime.convs.$MAN5EXT man/mime.convs.$MAN5EXT
f 0644 root sys $MANDIR/man5/mime.types.$MAN5EXT man/mime.types.$MAN5EXT
f 0644 root sys $MANDIR/man5/printers.conf.$MAN5EXT man/printers.conf.$MAN5EXT

f 0644 root sys $MANDIR/man7/backend.$MAN7EXT man/backend.$MAN7EXT
f 0644 root sys $MANDIR/man7/filter.$MAN7EXT man/filter.$MAN7EXT

f 0644 root sys $AMANDIR/man$MAN8DIR/accept.$MAN8EXT man/accept.$MAN8EXT
l 0644 root sys $AMANDIR/man$MAN8DIR/reject.$MAN8EXT accept.$MAN8EXT
f 0644 root sys $AMANDIR/man$MAN8DIR/cupsaddsmb.$MAN8EXT man/cupsaddsmb.$MAN8EXT
f 0644 root sys $AMANDIR/man$MAN8DIR/cups-polld.$MAN8EXT man/cups-polld.$MAN8EXT
f 0644 root sys $AMANDIR/man$MAN8DIR/cupsd.$MAN8EXT man/cupsd.$MAN8EXT
f 0644 root sys $AMANDIR/man$MAN8DIR/cupsenable.$MAN8EXT man/cupsenable.$MAN8EXT
l 0644 root sys $AMANDIR/man$MAN8DIR/cupsdisable.$MAN8EXT cupsenable.$MAN8EXT
f 0644 root sys $AMANDIR/man$MAN8DIR/lpadmin.$MAN8EXT man/lpadmin.$MAN8EXT
f 0644 root sys $AMANDIR/man$MAN8DIR/lpc.$MAN8EXT man/lpc.$MAN8EXT
f 0644 root sys $AMANDIR/man$MAN8DIR/lpinfo.$MAN8EXT man/lpinfo.$MAN8EXT
f 0644 root sys $AMANDIR/man$MAN8DIR/lpmove.$MAN8EXT man/lpmove.$MAN8EXT

%subpackage devel
f 0644 root sys $MANDIR/man1/cups-config.$MAN1EXT man/cups-config.$MAN1EXT

%subpackage lpd
d 0755 root sys $AMANDIR/man$MAN8DIR -
f 0644 root sys $AMANDIR/man$MAN8DIR/cups-lpd.$MAN8EXT man/cups-lpd.$MAN8EXT
%subpackage
```

Startup Script

The CUPS startup script is last and specifies a script name of
`cups`. Startup and shutdown scripts will be created with the
(default) names `S99cups` and `K00cups`, respectively.

```
%system all
i 0555 root sys cups init/cups.sh
```

A - GNU General Public License

GNU GENERAL PUBLIC LICENSE
Version 2, June 1991

GNU GENERAL PUBLIC LICENSE
TERMS AND CONDITIONS FOR COPYING,
DISTRIBUTION AND MODIFICATION

0. This License applies to any program or other work which
contains a notice placed by the copyright holder saying it
may be distributed under the terms of this General Public
License. The "Program", below, refers to any such program
or work, and a "work based on the Program" means either
the Program or any derivative work under copyright law:
that is to say, a work containing the Program or a portion of

it, either verbatim or with modifications and/or translated into another language. (Hereinafter, translation is included without limitation in the term "modification".) Each licensee is addressed as "you".

Activities other than copying, distribution and modification are not covered by this License; they are outside its scope. The act of running the Program is not restricted, and the output from the Program is covered only if its contents constitute a work based on the Program (independent of having been made by running the Program). Whether that is true depends on what the Program does.

1. You may copy and distribute verbatim copies of the Program's source code as you receive it, in any medium, provided that you conspicuously and appropriately publish on each copy an appropriate copyright notice and disclaimer of warranty; keep intact all the notices that refer to this License and to the absence of any warranty; and give any other recipients of the Program a copy of this License along with the Program.

You may charge a fee for the physical act of transferring a copy, and you may at your option offer warranty protection in exchange for a fee.

2. You may modify your copy or copies of the Program or any portion of it, thus forming a work based on the Program, and copy and distribute such modifications or work under the terms of Section 1 above, provided that you also meet all of these conditions:

> a. You must cause the modified files to carry prominent notices stating that you changed the files and the date of any change.

> b. You must cause any work that you distribute or publish, that in whole or in part contains or is derived from the Program or any part thereof, to be licensed as a whole at no charge to all third parties under the terms of this License.

c. If the modified program normally reads commands interactively when run, you must cause it, when started running for such interactive use in the most ordinary way, to print or display an announcement including an appropriate copyright notice and a notice that there is no warranty (or else, saying that you provide a warranty) and that users may redistribute the program under these conditions, and telling the user how to view a copy of this License. (Exception: if the Program itself is interactive but does not normally print such an announcement, your work based on the Program is not required to print an announcement.)

These requirements apply to the modified work as a whole. If identifiable sections of that work are not derived from the Program, and can be reasonably considered independent and separate works in themselves, then this License, and its terms, do not apply to those sections when you distribute them as separate works. But when you distribute the same sections as part of a whole which is a work based on the Program, the distribution of the whole must be on the terms of this License, whose permissions for other licensees extend to the entire whole, and thus to each and every part regardless of who wrote it.

Thus, it is not the intent of this section to claim rights or contest your rights to work written entirely by you; rather, the intent is to exercise the right to control the distribution of derivative or collective works based on the Program.

In addition, mere aggregation of another work not based on the Program with the Program (or with a work based on the Program) on a volume of a storage or distribution medium does not bring the other work under the scope of this License.

3. You may copy and distribute the Program (or a work based on it, under Section 2) in object code or executable form under the terms of Sections 1 and 2 above provided that you also do one of the following:

a. Accompany it with the complete corresponding machine-readable source code, which must be distributed under the terms of Sections 1 and 2 above on a medium customarily used for software interchange; or,

b. Accompany it with a written offer, valid for at least three years, to give any third party, for a charge no more than your cost of physically performing source distribution, a complete machine-readable copy of the corresponding source code, to be distributed under the terms of Sections 1 and 2 above on a medium customarily used for software interchange; or,

c. Accompany it with the information you received as to the offer to distribute corresponding source code. (This alternative is allowed only for noncommercial distribution and only if you received the program in object code or executable form with such an offer, in accord with Subsection b above.)

The source code for a work means the preferred form of the work for making modifications to it. For an executable work, complete source code means all the source code for all modules it contains, plus any associated interface definition files, plus the scripts used to control compilation and installation of the executable. However, as a special exception, the source code distributed need not include anything that is normally distributed (in either source or binary form) with the major components (compiler, kernel, and so on) of the operating system on which the executable runs, unless that component itself accompanies the executable.

If distribution of executable or object code is made by offering access to copy from a designated place, then offering equivalent access to copy the source code from the same place counts as distribution of the source code, even though third parties are not compelled to copy the source along with the object code.

4. You may not copy, modify, sublicense, or distribute the Program except as expressly provided under this License. Any attempt otherwise to copy, modify, sublicense or distribute the Program is void, and will automatically terminate your rights under this License. However, parties who have received copies, or rights, from you under this License will not have their licenses terminated so long as such parties remain in full compliance.

5. You are not required to accept this License, since you have not signed it. However, nothing else grants you permission to modify or distribute the Program or its derivative works. These actions are prohibited by law if you do not accept this License. Therefore, by modifying or distributing the Program (or any work based on the Program), you indicate your acceptance of this License to do so, and all its terms and conditions for copying, distributing or modifying the Program or works based on it.

6. Each time you redistribute the Program (or any work based on the Program), the recipient automatically receives a license from the original licensor to copy, distribute or modify the Program subject to these terms and conditions. You may not impose any further restrictions on the recipients' exercise of the rights granted herein. You are not responsible for enforcing compliance by third parties to this License.

7. If, as a consequence of a court judgment or allegation of patent infringement or for any other reason (not limited to patent issues), conditions are imposed on you (whether by court order, agreement or otherwise) that contradict the conditions of this License, they do not excuse you from the conditions of this License. If you cannot distribute so as to satisfy simultaneously your obligations under this License and any other pertinent obligations, then as a consequence you may not distribute the Program at all. For example, if a patent license would not permit royalty-free redistribution of the Program by all those who receive copies directly or indirectly through you, then the only way you could satisfy both it and this License would be to refrain entirely from distribution of the Program.

If any portion of this section is held invalid or unenforceable under any particular circumstance, the balance of the section is intended to apply and the section as a whole is intended to apply in other circumstances.

It is not the purpose of this section to induce you to infringe any patents or other property right claims or to contest validity of any such claims; this section has the sole purpose of protecting the integrity of the free software distribution system, which is implemented by public license practices. Many people have made generous contributions to the wide range of software distributed through that system in reliance on consistent application of that system; it is up to the author/donor to decide if he or she is willing to distribute software through any other system and a licensee cannot impose that choice.

This section is intended to make thoroughly clear what is believed to be a consequence of the rest of this License.

8. If the distribution and/or use of the Program is restricted in certain countries either by patents or by copyrighted interfaces, the original copyright holder who places the Program under this License may add an explicit geographical distribution limitation excluding those countries, so that distribution is permitted only in or among countries not thus excluded. In such case, this License incorporates the limitation as if written in the body of this License.

9. The Free Software Foundation may publish revised and/or new versions of the General Public License from time to time. Such new versions will be similar in spirit to the present version, but may differ in detail to address new problems or concerns.

Each version is given a distinguishing version number. If the Program specifies a version number of this License which applies to it and "any later version", you have the option of following the terms and conditions either of that version or of any later version published by the Free Software Foundation. If the Program does not specify a version number of this License, you may choose any version ever published by the Free Software Foundation.

10. If you wish to incorporate parts of the Program into other free programs whose distribution conditions are different, write to the author to ask for permission. For software which is copyrighted by the Free Software Foundation, write to the Free Software Foundation; we sometimes make exceptions for this. Our decision will be guided by the two goals of preserving the free status of all derivatives of our free software and of promoting the sharing and reuse of software generally.

NO WARRANTY

11. BECAUSE THE PROGRAM IS LICENSED FREE OF CHARGE, THERE IS NO WARRANTY FOR THE PROGRAM, TO THE EXTENT PERMITTED BY APPLICABLE LAW. EXCEPT WHEN OTHERWISE STATED IN WRITING THE COPYRIGHT HOLDERS AND/OR OTHER PARTIES PROVIDE THE PROGRAM "AS IS" WITHOUT WARRANTY OF ANY KIND, EITHER EXPRESSED OR IMPLIED, INCLUDING, BUT NOT LIMITED TO, THE IMPLIED WARRANTIES OF MERCHANTABILITY AND FITNESS FOR A PARTICULAR PURPOSE. THE ENTIRE RISK AS TO THE QUALITY AND PERFORMANCE OF THE PROGRAM IS WITH YOU. SHOULD THE PROGRAM PROVE DEFECTIVE, YOU ASSUME THE COST OF ALL NECESSARY SERVICING, REPAIR OR CORRECTION.

12. IN NO EVENT UNLESS REQUIRED BY APPLICABLE LAW OR AGREED TO IN WRITING WILL ANY COPYRIGHT HOLDER, OR ANY OTHER PARTY WHO MAY MODIFY AND/OR REDISTRIBUTE THE PROGRAM AS PERMITTED ABOVE, BE LIABLE TO YOU FOR DAMAGES, INCLUDING ANY GENERAL, SPECIAL, INCIDENTAL OR CONSEQUENTIAL DAMAGES ARISING OUT OF THE USE OR INABILITY TO USE THE PROGRAM (INCLUDING BUT NOT LIMITED TO LOSS OF DATA OR DATA BEING RENDERED INACCURATE OR LOSSES SUSTAINED BY YOU OR THIRD PARTIES OR A FAILURE OF THE PROGRAM TO OPERATE WITH ANY OTHER PROGRAMS), EVEN IF SUCH HOLDER OR OTHER PARTY HAS BEEN ADVISED OF THE POSSIBILITY OF SUCH DAMAGES.

END OF TERMS AND CONDITIONS

HOW TO APPLY THESE TERMS TO YOUR NEW PROGRAMS

If you develop a new program, and you want it to be of the greatest possible use to the public, the best way to achieve this is to make it free software which everyone can redistribute and change under these terms.

To do so, attach the following notices to the program. It is safest to attach them to the start of each source file to most effectively convey the exclusion of warranty; and each file should have at least the "copyright" line and a pointer to where the full notice is found.

one line to give the program's name and an idea of what it does.
Copyright (C) *yyyy   name of author*

This program is free software; you can redistribute it and/or modify it under the terms of the GNU General Public License as published by the Free Software Foundation; either version 2 of the License, or (at your option) any later version.

This program is distributed in the hope that it will be useful, but WITHOUT ANY WARRANTY; without even the implied warranty of MERCHANTABILITY or FITNESS FOR A PARTICULAR PURPOSE. See the GNU General Public License for more details.

You should have received a copy of the GNU General Public License along with this program; if not, write to the Free Software Foundation, Inc., 59 Temple Place - Suite 330, Boston, MA 02111-1307, USA.

Also add information on how to contact you by electronic and paper mail.

If the program is interactive, make it output a short notice like this when it starts in an interactive mode:

Gnomovision version 69, Copyright (C) *year name of author*
Gnomovision comes with ABSOLUTELY NO WARRANTY; for details type `show w'.  This is free software, and you are welcome to redistribute it under certain conditions; type `show c' for details.

The hypothetical commands `show w'` and `show c'` should show the appropriate parts of the General Public License. Of course, the commands you use may be called something other than `show w'` and `show c'`; they could even be mouse-clicks or menu items--whatever suits your program.

You should also get your employer (if you work as a programmer) or your school, if any, to sign a "copyright disclaimer" for the program, if necessary. Here is a sample; alter the names:

```
Yoyodyne, Inc., hereby disclaims all copyright
interest in the program `Gnomovision'
(which makes passes at compilers) written
by James Hacker.
```

signature of Ty Coon, 1 April 1989
Ty Coon, President of Vice

B - Command Reference

epm(1)

Name

epm - create software packages.

Synopsis

epm [-a *architecture*] [-f *format*] [-g] [-k] [-m *name*] [
-n[mrs]] [-s *setup.xpm*] [--depend] [--help] [--keep-files
] [--output-dir *directory*] [--setup-image *setup.xpm*] [
--setup-program */foo/bar/setup*] [--setup-types *setup.types*
] [-v] [*name=value ... name=value*] product [*listfile*]

Description

epm generates software packages complete with
installation, removal, and (if necessary) patch scripts. Unless
otherwise specified, the files required for *product* are read
from a file named "*product*.list".

The *-a* option ("architecture") specifies the actual
architecture for the software. Without this option the generic
processor architecture is used ("intel", "sparc", "mips", etc.)

The *-f* option ("format") specifies the distribution format:

aix
>   Generate an AIX distribution suitable for installation
>   on an AIX system.

bsd
>   Generate a BSD distribution suitable for installation
>   on a FreeBSD, NetBSD, or OpenBSD system.

deb
>   Generate a Debian distribution suitable for
>   installation on a Debian Linux system.

inst, tardist
>   Generate an IRIX distribution suitable for installation
>   on an system running IRIX.

lsb, lsb-signed

> Generate RPM packages for LSB-conforming systems. The lsb-signed format uses the GPG private key you have defined in the ~/.rpmmacros file.

native

> Generate an native distribution. This uses *rpm* for Linux, *inst* for IRIX, *pkg* for Solaris, *swinstall* for HP-UX, *bsd* for FreeBSD, NetBSD, and OpenBSD, and *osx* for MacOS X. All other operating systems default to the *portable* format.

osx

> Generate a MacOS X software package.

pkg

> Generate an AT&T software package. These are used primarily under Solaris.

portable

> Generate a portable distribution based on shell scripts and tar files. The resulting distribution is installed and removed the same way on all operating systems. [default]

rpm, rpm-signed

> Generate a Red Hat Package Manager ("RPM") distribution suitable for installation on a Red Hat Linux system. The rpm-signed format uses the GPG private key you have defined in the ~/.rpmmacros file.

setld

> Generate a Tru64 (setld) software distribution.

slackware

> Generate a Slackware Linux software distribution.

swinstall, depot

> Generate a HP-UX software distribution.

Executable files in the distribution are normally stripped of debugging information when packaged. To disable this functionality use the *-g* option.

Intermediate (spec, etc.) files used to create the distribution are normally removed after the distribution is created. The *-k* option keeps these files in the distribution directory.

The *-s* and *--setup-image* options ("setup") include the ESP Software Wizard with the specified GIF or XPM image file with the distribution. This option is currently only supported by portable and RPM distributions.

The *--setup-program* option specifies the setup executable to use with the distribution. This option is currently only supported by portable distributions.

The *--setup-types* option specifies the *setup.types* file to include with the distribution. This option is currently only supported by portable distributions.

The *--output-dir* option specifies the directory to place output file into. The default directory is based on the operating system, version, and architecture.

The *-v* option ("verbose") increases the amount of information that is reported. Use multiple v's for more verbose output.

The *--depend* option lists the dependent (source) files for all files in the package.

Distributions normally are named "product-version-system-release-machine.ext" and "product-version-system-release-machine-patch.ext" (for patch distributions.) The "system-release-machine" information can be customized or eliminated using the *-n* option with the appropriate trailing letters. Using *-n* by itself will remove the "system-release-machine" string from the filename entirely. The "system-release-machine" information can also be customized by using the *-m* option with an arbitrary string.

Debian, IRIX, portable, and Red Hat distributions use the extensions ".deb", ".tardist", "tar.gz", and ".rpm" respectively.

List Files

The EPM list file format is now described in the *epm.list(5)* man page.

Known Bugs

EPM does not currently support generation of IRIX software patches.

See Also

epminstall(1) - add a directory, file, or symlink to a list file
mkepmlist(1) - make an epm list file from a directory
epm.list(5) - epm list file format
setup(1) - graphical setup program for the esp package manager

Copyright

epminstall(1)

Name

epminstall - add a directory, file, or symlink to a list file.

Synopsis

epminstall *options* file1 file2 ... fileN directory
epminstall *options* file1 file2
epminstall *options* -d directory1 directory2 ... directoryN

Description

epminstall adds or replaces a directory, file, or symlink in a list file. The default list file is "epm.list" and can be overridden using the *EPMLIST* environment variable or the *--list-file* option.

Entries are either added to the end of the list file or replaced in-line. Comments, directives, and variable declarations in the list file are preserved.

Options

epminstall recognizes the standard Berkeley *install* command options:

-b

> Make a backup of existing files (ignored, default for EPM.)

-c

> BSD old compatibility mode (ignored.)

-g *group*

> Set the group owner of the file or directory to *group*. The default group is "sys".

-m *mode*

> Set the permissions of the file or directory to *mode*. The default permissions are 0755 for directories and executable files and 0644 for non-executable files.

-o *owner*

> Set the owner of the file or directory to *owner*. The default owner is "root".

-s

> Strip the files (ignored, default for EPM.)

--list-file *filename.list*

> Specify the list file to update.

See Also

epm(1) - create software packages
mkepmlist(1) - make an epm list file from a directory
epm.list(5) - epm list file format

Copyright

mkepmlist(1)

Name

mkepmlist - make an epm list file from a directory.

Synopsis

mkepmlist [-g *group*] [-u *user*] [--prefix *directory*] *directory* [... *directory*]

Description

mkepmlist recursively generates file list entries for files, links, and directories. The file list is send to the standard output.

The -*g* option overrides the group ownership of the files in the specified directories with the specified group name.

The -*u* option overrides the user ownership of the files in the specified directories with the specified user name.

The --*prefix* option adds the specified directory to the destination path. For example, if you installed files to "/opt/foo" and wanted to build a distribution that installed the files in "/usr/local", the following command would generate a file list that is installed in "/usr/local":

```
mkepmlist --prefix=/usr/local /opt/foo >foo.list
```

See Also

epm(1) - create software packages
epminstall(1) - add a directory, file, or symlink to a list file
epm.list(5) - epm list file format

Copyright

setup(1)

Name

setup - graphical setup program for the esp package manager

Synopsis

setup [*directory*]

Description

setup provides a graphical installation interface for EPM-generated portable installation packages. It presents a step-by-step dialog for collecting a list of packages to install and accepting any license agreements for those packages.

setup searches for products in the current directory or the directory specified on the command-line.

Installation Types

The default type of installation is "custom". That is, users will be able to select from the list of products and install them.

setup also supports other types of installations. The *setup.types* file, if present, defines the other installation types.

See Also

epm(1) - create software packages.
setup.types(5) - epm gui setup types file format.

Copyright

Copyright 1999-2007 by Easy Software Products, All Rights Reserved.

This program is free software; you can redistribute it and/or modify it under the terms of the GNU General Public License as published by the Free Software Foundation; either version 2, or (at your option) any later version.

This program is distributed in the hope that it will be useful, but WITHOUT ANY WARRANTY; without even the implied warranty of MERCHANTABILITY or FITNESS FOR A PARTICULAR PURPOSE. See the GNU General Public License for more details.

Software Distribution Using the ESP Package Manager

C - List File Reference

This appendix provides a complete reference for the EPM list file and setup types formats.

The EPM List File Format

Each *EPM* product has an associated list file that describes the files to include with the product. Comment lines begin with the "#" character and are ignored. All other non-blank lines must begin with a letter, dollar sign ("$"), or the percent sign ("%").

List File Directives

The following list describes all of the list file directives supported by *EPM*:

$name=value

> Sets the named variable to *value*. **Note:** Variables set in the list file are overridden by variables specified on the command-line or in the current environment.

%copyright *copyright notice*

> Sets the copyright notice for the file.

%description *description text*

> Adds a line of descriptive text to the distribution. Multiple lines are supported.

%format *format [... format]*

> Uses following files and directives only if the distribution format is the same as *format*.

%format !*format [... format]*

> Uses following files and directives only if the distribution format is not the same as *format*.

%include *filename*

> Includes files listed in *filename*.

%incompat *product*
%incompat *filename*

> Indicates that this product is incompatible with the named product or file.

%if *variable [... variable]*
%if *!variable [... variable]*
%ifdef *variable [... variable]*
%ifdef *!variable [... variable]*
%elseif *variable [... variable]*
%elseif *!variable [... variable]*
%elseifdef *variable [... variable]*
%elseifdef *!variable [... variable]*
%else
%endif

> Conditionally includes lines in the list file. The *%if* lines include the lines that follow if the named variables are (not) defined with a value. The *%ifdef* lines include the lines that follow if the named variables are (not) defined with any value. These conditional lines cannot be nested.

%install *script or program*

> Specifies a script or program to be run after all files are installed. (This has been obsoleted by the %postinstall directive)

%license *license file*

> Specifies the file to display as the software license.

%packager *name of packager*

> Specifies the name of the packager.

%patch *script or program*

> Specifies a script or program to be run after all files are patched. (This has been obsoleted by the %postpatch directive)

%postinstall *script or program*
%postinstall *<scriptfile*
%postinstall *<<string*

> Specifies a script or program to be run after all files are installed.

%postpatch *script or program*
%postpatch *<scriptfile*
%postpatch *<<string*

> Specifies a script or program to be run after all files are patched.

%postremove *script or program*
%postremove *<scriptfile*
%postremove *<<string*

> Specifies a script or program to be run after removing files.

%preinstall *script or program*
%preinstall *<scriptfile*
%preinstall *<<string*

> Specifies a script or program to be run before all files are installed.

%prepatch *script or program*
%prepatch *<scriptfile*
%prepatch *<<string*

> Specifies a script or program to be run before all files are patched.

%preremove *script or program*
%preremove *<scriptfile*
%preremove *<<string*

> Specifies a script or program to be run before removing files.

%product *product name*

> Specifies the product name.

%provides *product name*

> Indicates that this product provides the named dependency.

%readme *readme file*

> Specifies a README file to be included in the distribution.

%remove *script or program*

> Specifies a script or program to be run before removing files. (This has been obsoleted by the %preremove directive)

%release *number*

> Specifies the release or build number of a product (defaults to 0).

%replaces *product*

> Indicates that this product replaces the named product.

%requires *product*
%requires *filename*

> Indicates that this product requires the named product or file.

%system *system[-release] [... system[-release]]*

> Specifies that the following files should only be used for the specified operating systems and releases.

%system !*system[-release]* [*... system[-release]]*

>   Specifies that the following files should not be used for the specified operating systems and releases.

%system all

>   Specifies that the following files are applicable to all operating systems.

%vendor *vendor or author name*

>   Specifies the vendor or author of the product.

%version *version number*

>   Specifies the version number of the product.

c *mode user group destination source*
C *mode user group destination source*

>   Specifies a configuration file for installation. The second form specifies that the file has changed or is new and should be included as part of a patch. Configuration files are installed as "destination.N" if the destination already exists.

d *mode user group destination -*
D *mode user group destination -*

>   Specifies a directory should be created when installing the software. The second form specifies that the directory is new and should be included as part of a patch.

f *mode user group destination source [nostrip()]*
F *mode user group destination source [nostrip()]*

> Specifies a file for installation. The second form specifies that the file has changed or is new and should be included as part of a patch. If the "nostrip()" option is included, the file will not be stripped before the installation is created.

f *mode user group destination source/pattern [nostrip()]*
F *mode user group destination source/pattern [nostrip()]*

> Specifies one or more files for installation using shell wildcard patterns. The second form specifies that the files have changed or are new and should be included as part of a patch. If the "nostrip()" option is included, the file will not be stripped before the installation is created.

i *mode user group service-name source ["options"]*
I *mode user group service-name source ["options"]*

> Specifies an initialization script for installation. The second form specifies that the file has changed or is new and should be included as part of a patch. Initialization scripts are stored in */etc/software/init.d* and are linked to the appropriate system-specific directories for run levels 0, 2, 3, and 5. Initialization scripts **must** accept at least the *start* and *stop* commands. The optional *options* following the source filename can be any of the following:

order(*string*)
> Specifies the relative startup order compared to the required and used system functions. Supported values include First, Early, None, Late, and

Last (OSX only).

provides(*name(s)*)

Specifies names of system functions
that are provided by this startup item
(OSX only).

requires(*name(s)*)

Specifies names of system functions
that are required by this startup item
(OSX only).

runlevels(*levels*)

Specifies the run levels to use.

start(*number*)

Specifies the starting sequence
number from 00 to 99.

stop(*number*)

Specifies the ending sequence number
from 00 to 99.

uses(*name(s)*)

Specifies names of system functions
that are used by this startup item (OSX
only).

l *mode user group destination source*
L *mode user group destination source*

Specifies a symbolic link in the installation.
The second form specifies that the link has
changed or is new and should be included as
part of a patch.

R *mode user group destination*

Specifies that the file is to be removed upon
patching. The *user* and *group* fields are
ignored. The *mode* field is only used to
determine if a check should be made for a
previous version of the file.

List Variables

EPM maintains a list of variables and their values which can be used to substitute values in the list file. These variables are imported from the current environment and taken from the command-line and list file as provided. Substitutions occur when the variable name is referenced with the dollar sign ($):

```
%postinstall <<EOF
echo What is your name:
read $$name
echo Your name is $$name
EOF

f 0555 root sys ${bindir}/foo foo
f 0555 root sys $datadir/foo/foo.dat foo.dat
```

Variable names can be surrounded by curly brackets (${name}) or alone ($name); without brackets the name is terminated by the first slash (/), dash (-), or whitespace. The dollar sign can be inserted using $$.

The setup.types File

The EPM **setup** program normally presents the user with a list of software products to install, which is called a "custom" software installation.

If a file called *setup.types* is present in the package directory, the user will instead be presented with a list of installation types. Each type has an associated product list which determines the products that are installed by default. If a type has no products associated with it, then it is treated as a custom installation and the user is presented with a list of packages to choose from.

The *setup.types* file is an ASCII text file consisting of type and product lines. Comments can be inserted by starting a line with the pound sign (#). Each installation type is defined by a line starting with the word TYPE. Products are defined by a line starting with the word INSTALL:

```
# Pre-select the user packages
TYPE Typical End-User Configuration
INSTALL foo
INSTALL foo-help

# Pre-select the developer packages
TYPE Typical Developer Configuration
INSTALL foo
INSTALL foo-help
INSTALL foo-devel
INSTALL foo-examples

# Allow the user to select packages
TYPE Custom Configuration
```

In the example above, three installation types are defined. Since the last type includes no products, the user will be presented with the full list of products to choose from.

D - Release Notes

This appendix lists the change log for each release of the EPM software.

Changes in EPM v4.2

- EPM now supports a %arch conditional directive (STR #27)
- EPM now uses hard links whenever possible instead of copying files for distribution (STR #21)
- EPM no longer puts files in /export in the root file set for AIX packages (STR #15)
- EPM did not work with newer versions of RPM (STR #23, STR #25)
- EPM did not clean up temporary files from Solaris packages (STR #20)
- Building Solaris gzip'd packages failed if the pkg.gz file already existed (STR #16)
- Fixed handling of %preremove and %postremove for AIX packages (STR #22)

- Fixed directory permissions in HP-UX packages (STR #24)
- Removed unnecessary quoting of "!" in filenames (STR #26)
- Added support for signed RPM packages (STR #19)
- Added support for inclusion of format-specific packaging files and directives via a %literal directive (STR #5)
- *BSD init scripts were not installed properly.
- EPM now displays a warning message when a variable is undefined (STR #10)
- *BSD dependencies on versioned packages are now specified correctly (STR #4)
- EPM now uses /usr/sbin/pkg_create on FreeBSD (STR #2)
- FreeBSD packages are now created with a .tbz extension (STR #1)
- FreeBSD packages incorrectly assumed that chown was installed in /bin (STR #3)
- Added support for an "lsb" package format which uses RPM with the LSB dependencies (STR #7)
- The configure script now supports a --with-archflags and no longer automatically builds universal binaries on Mac OS X.
- The epm program now automatically detects when the setup GUI is not available, displays a warning message, and then creates a non-GUI package.
- RPM packages did not map %replaces to Obsoletes:

Changes in EPM v4.1

- Mac OS X portable packages did not create a correct Uninstall application.
- The temporary package files for portable packages are now removed after creation of the .tar.gz file unless the -k (keep files) option is used.
- The RPM summary string for subpackages did not contain the first line of the package description as for other package formats.
- The setup and uninst GUIs now support installing and removing RPM packages.

- The setup GUI now confirms acceptance of all licenses prior to installing the first package.
- Subpackages are no longer automatically dependent on the main package.
- Multi-line descriptions were not embedded properly into portable package install/patch/remove scripts.
- Updated the setup and uninstall GUIs for a nicer look-n-feel.
- Mac OS X portable packages now show the proper name, version, and copyright for the packaged software instead of the EPM version and copyright...
- Fixed a problem with creation of Mac OS X metapackages with the latest Xcode.
- EPM now removes the individual .rpm and .deb files when creating a package with subpackages unless the -k option (keep files) is used.
- EPM now only warns about package names containing characters other than letters and numbers.
- EPM now generates disk images as well as a .tar.gz file when creating portable packages on Mac OS X.

Changes in EPM v4.0

- New subpackage support for creating multiple dependent packages or a combined package with selectable subpackages, depending on the package format.
- Added support for compressing the package files in portable packages (reduces disk space requirements on platforms that provide gzip...)
- Added support for custom platform names via the new "-m name" option.
- Added support for non-numeric %release values.
- Added new --depend option to list all of the source files that a package depends on.
- The setup GUI now sets the EPM_INSTALL_TYPE environment variable to the value of the selected TYPE line in the setup.types file.
- Fixed NetBSD and OpenBSD packaging support - no longer use FreeBSD-specific extensions to pkg_create

on those variants.
- Fixed PowerPC platform support for RPM and Debian packages.
- Many fixes to AIX package support.
- Tru64 packages with init scripts now work when installing for the first time.
- RPM file dependencies should now work properly.
- Portable product names containing spaces will now display properly.

www.ingramcontent.com/pod-product-compliance
Lightning Source LLC
Chambersburg PA
CBHW022115170526
45157CB00004B/1655